The Antarctic Warms Up

COLOURED VERSION

CHILDREN SAVING OUR PLANET SERIES

CAROL SUTTERS

AuthorHouse™ UK
1663 Liberty Drive
Bloomington, IN 47403 USA
www.authorhouse.co.uk
UK TFN: 0800 0148641 (Toll Free inside the UK)
UK Local: 02036 956322 (+44 20 3695 6322 from outside the UK)

Because of the dynamic nature of the Internet, any web addresses or links contained in this book may have changed since publication and may no longer be valid. The views expressed in this work are solely those of the author and do not necessarily reflect the views of the publisher, and the publisher hereby disclaims any responsibility for them.

Any people depicted in stock imagery provided by Getty Images are models, and such images are being used for illustrative purposes only.
Certain stock imagery © Getty Images.

This book is printed on acid-free paper.

ISBN: 978-1-6655-8799-0 (sc)
ISBN: 978-1-6655-8800-3 (e)

Library of Congress Control Number: 2021906671

Print information available on the last page.

Published by AuthorHouse 04/24/2021

authorHOUSE®

Mum suggests, "*We should watch a programme about the Antarctic ice sheets melting.*" "*Where is this?*" asks Kate.

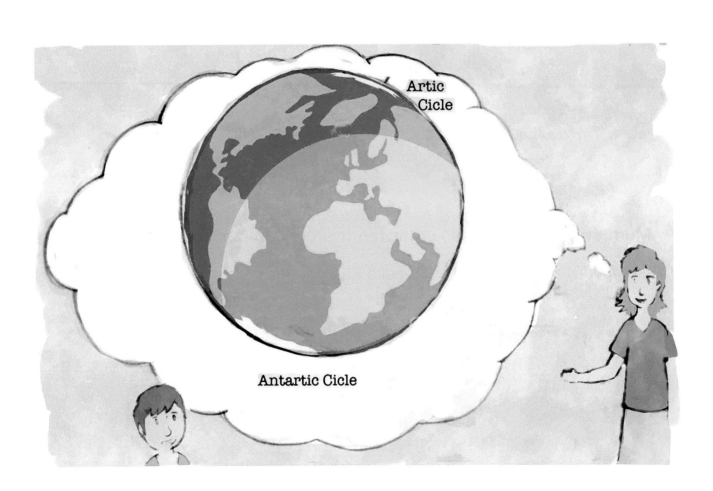

"It is at the South Pole," says Mum. "The North Pole is called the Arctic circle and is affected in the same way."

The programme reported that the Antarctic is the most southern point on the earth and it is a sheet of ice. It is known for being the highest, driest, coldest and windiest continent on earth. Scientists monitor the ice melting there using satellites in space.

"Why is this important?" asks Tom. Mum replies, "Some of the ice at the Antarctic has been there for millions of years. However, as the programme states there is evidence that parts of the Antarctic are warming up three times faster than the rest of the world."

"Scientists believe that human causes of global warming, rather than just natural causes, are accelerating ice loss from West Antarctica.

This may be related to climate changes thousands of miles away in the tropics in the west Pacific Ocean. Regional winds caused by differences in temperature between the centre at the Equator and the south pole are driving changes. Westerly warm winds reach the Antarctic ice shelf and cause changes in the flow of warm water. The result is that warm water is getting under the ice. This is melting the ice shelves from beneath, causing the ice shelves to break up."

Mum continues, "*In 2020 weather stations recorded the highest ever temperatures in the Antarctic. Scientists have also found a lot of green and red algae growing in the melting coastal Antarctic snow. This has only happened due to climate change. The ice shelves both in the north and south poles are very important.*

The ice sheets are very, very deep and the area is home to many types of animals and plants even though it all looks like ice. Animals we would find there include: penguins, whales, walruses, sea birds and there are lots of fishes and tiny organisms in the waters below."

"Antarctica is also important in the carbon cycle. There are millions of species of phytoplankton that appear green and yellow in the oceans and ice. These are algae that use the carbon dioxide and water to make oxygen and energy. They remove carbon dioxide from surface water. They are eaten by zooplankton, which are often eaten by larger animals, but many just die and sink into to the sea bottom. This dead marine life becomes sediment. The process transports carbon down to the depths so it can be stored for hundreds of years. This is a very effective carbon pump. But, these organisms are being replaced by by others. Also they are being invaded by microplastics, introduced by humans. Life is the Antarctic may soak up twice as much carbon as the whole of the Amazon rain Forest."

"It is important as we must maintain the balance of temperature in different parts of the world, to maintain the ecosystems and animals and plants that live there."

"Increasing carbon dioxide levels are putting a lot more heat into the atmosphere and the oceans and making them more acidic. Heat is energy, and energy drives the weather and ocean currents. As we increase the amount of energy in the system, big global processes are going to change. When polar ice melts it contributes massively to the amount of water in the world seas. Therefore, as the polar ice melts so the sea level rises and this can be catastrophic in some coastal cities. This is occurring in Bangladesh. The programme reported that the A68 iceberg which broke off the Antarctic peninsula in 2017 has just virtually gone. This is a catastrophe."

What did we learn today? (tick the box if you understood and agree)

☐ The Antarctic ice sheets, together with the Arctic circle, are key to preserving climate, the seas and the world in which we live.

☐ Phytoplankton in oceans are very effective at removing carbon dioxide from the atmosphere.

☐ Greenhouse gases such as carbon dioxide, cause warming of water currents and temperatures which can cause the ice to melt.

☐ Melting ice sheets can cause sea levels to rise and coastal homes and towns may be flooded or even lost into the seas.

Read about how Kate and Tom leant about a climate change tipping point in the Canada Catastrophe in Book 14.

Children Saving our Planet Series

Books

1. **Tom and Kate Go to Westminster**

2. **Kate and Tom Learn About Fossil Fuels**

3. **Tom and Kate Chose Green Carbon**

4. **Tress and Deforestation**

5. **Our Neighbourhood Houses**

6. **Our Neighbourhood Roads**

7. **Shopping at the Farm Shop**

8. **Travelling to a Holiday by the Sea**

9. **Picnic at the Seaside on Holiday**

10. **The Oceans and Coral**

11. **Our Carbon Footprint**

12. **Fire Fire**

13. **The Antarctic Warms Up**

14. **The Canada Catastrophe**

15. **The Coronavirus and saving the Planet**

16. **The Children's Rebellion and Climate Change**

These series of simple books explain the landmark importance of Children's participation in the Extinction rebellion protest. Children actively want to encourage and support adults to urgently tackle both the Climate and the Biodiversity emergencies. The booklets enable children at an early age to understand some of the scientific principles that are affecting the destruction of the planet. If global political and economic systems fail to address the climate emergency, the responsibility will rest upon children to save the Planet for themselves.

This series is dedicated to

Theodore, Aria and Ophelia.

Printed in the United States
by Baker & Taylor Publisher Services